THE

THE Great Opera Stars IN HISTORIC PHOTOGRAPHS

343 Portraits from the 1850s to the 1940s

Edited by
JAMES CAMNER

DOVER PUBLICATIONS, INC.
NEW YORK

Published in Canada by General Publishing Company, Ltd., 30 Lesmill Road, Don Mills, Toronto, Ontario.
Published in the United Kingdom by Constable and Company, Ltd., 10 Orange Street, London WC2H 7EG.

The Great Opera Stars in Historic Photographs: 343 Portraits from the 1850s to the 1940s is a new work, first published by Dover Publications, Inc., in 1978.

International Standard Book Number: 0-486-23575-0
Library of Congress Catalog Card Number: 77-86260

Manufactured in the United States of America
Dover Publications, Inc.
180 Varick Street
New York, N.Y. 10014

FRONTISPIECE: ADELINA PATTI as Marguerite in Gounod's *Faust*. See also illustration No. 25 and caption.

PICTURE CREDITS

Editor and publisher are grateful to the following lenders of photographs:

Michael Bavar: Illus. 7, 15, 19, 20, 24, 42, 58, 66, 82, 94, 98, 103, 114, 115, 118, 131, 142, 159, 161, 165, 187, 188, 197, 200, 212, 227, 233, 236, 238, 240, 252, 256, 267, 278, 279, 289, 290, 300, 307, 312, 327, 329.
Robert Connally: 1, 3, 5, 8, 9, 17, 32, 34, 68, 174, 215.
Norman Crider (Ballet Shop): 22, 31, 63.
Anna Sosenko (Autographs): 65, 75, 97, 99, 101, 113, 117, 129, 237, 266, 275.

All other photographs are from the collection of James Camner and the files of La Scala Autographs.

INTRODUCTION

This is a book devoted to photographs of opera singers: not operas, not opera houses, but the stars of opera, the personalities who bring operas to life and to whom audiences and composers owe an everlasting debt of gratitude. In assembling the photos, we tried to find as many examples of great and near-great singers as possible, dating back as early as possible. In general, we did not include singers whose careers began after World War II. If this eliminated some great singers, it also cut out some possible arguments. Certainly the emphasis is on the classic singers, who, as just about everyone will concede, were "Golden Age," and whose photos are usually hard to find and, in some cases, are unpublished as well. Unfortunately, even with this cut-off, it was not possible to include all deserving singers, but either pictures were unavailable or the available ones were unsatisfactory. All the illustrations in this book were chosen for their fine visual quality. Some singers are represented by two or more photos because of especial pictorial interest. In the case of such a truly photogenic singer as Geraldine Farrar (Nos. 182–186), it was quite difficult to limit the selection to five pictures!

This book may contain the greatest number of photos of opera singers ever assembled in one publication. We were very gratified to be able to include actual photos of singers of such a distant era as the early Romantic period. With Tamburini (No. 1) and Mario (No. 2) we are brought face to face with favorite singers of Bellini and Donizetti. Two very unusual photos are those of Etelka Gerster (No. 51) and Emma Eames (No. 86). As opposed to the typical studio poses, these are stage poses in a stage setting. The Gerster in particular really evokes a feeling of the nineteenth-century theater.

One could point out some outstanding characteristic of each of the photos, as they all bring out some truth about a singer. For example, Ernestine Schumann-Heink's sweetness is shown in No. 79. An extraordinary performer on records, Conchita Supervia reveals a similar charm in her photo (No. 283). There is an especially interesting contrast between the two photos of Leo Slezak (Nos. 127 and 128), one a gentle, humorous picture taken in private life and the other a pose in costume as the crazed Otello. The photos of Francisco d'Andrade (No. 65), Victor Maurel (No. 38) and Ezio Pinza (Nos. 259 and 262) all show why they were considered premier Don Giovannis.

There are some rare photographs of singers who are perhaps less familiar to opera devotees in America. Léon Melchissédec (No. 23), Gabrielle Krauss (No. 24), Lucienne Bréval (No. 93) and Léon Escalaïs (No. 66) were all glories of the Paris Opéra. Catherine Mastio (No. 146), also of the Paris Opéra, had a lovely voice but lovely voices abounded in her day and she is little known. Jean de Reszke and Caruso so dominate their eras in retrospect that many truly great tenors are not as well remembered as their accomplishments deserve. Thus, picures of Angelo Masini (No. 28), the outstanding Italian tenor of his day; Nikolai Figner (No. 55), the outstanding Russian tenor; and Hermann Jadlowker (No. 157), the outstanding German tenor, have not been as sought after or preserved with the same zeal. Even more familiar singers, such as Feodor Chaliapin (No. 125) and Titta Ruffo (No. 159), are shown here in rare poses.

Many of the photos are autographed. Some readers may object to the image being marred in this way, but most will probably agree that the signature enhances the picture, making it more personal and appealing. In one instance, a photo of one singer in the book has been inscribed to a colleague also in the book: Fernando De Lucia (No. 68) to Barbara Marchisio (No. 14). Autograph collectors will find the reproduced signatures useful for authentication of their own collection and for identification of illegibile scrawls such as Leo Slezak's (No. 128).

In many cases, the reader will be able to match the face with a recorded voice and in this way have a complete documentation of the singer. And in the case of singers who retired before the age of recordings, the pictures may at least be matched with their legends.

The book was immeasurably enriched by the lenders named in the list of picture credits, to whom we extend heartfelt thanks.

James Camner

THE *Great Opera Stars* IN HISTORIC PHOTOGRAPHS

343 Portraits from the 1850s to the 1940s

1

2

3

1. ANTONIO TAMBURINI (1800–1876), Italian baritone. One of the superb members of the Parisian Théâtre-Italien company in the 1830s and 1840s, he created the role of Malatesta in Donizetti's *Don Pasquale*. (Photo: L. Reali) 2. GIOVANNI MARIO (Mario Cavaliere di Candia, 1810–1883, husband of Giulia Grisi), Italian tenor. In the 1840s he replaced Rubini in the famous "quartet" at the Théâtre-Italien (the others were Giulia Grisi, Luigi Lablache and Tamburini), creating the role of Ernesto in *Don Pasquale*. 3. ENRICO TAMBERLI(C)K (1820–1889), Italian tenor. He was the original Don Alvaro in Verdi's *La Forza del destino* in 1862. (Photo: Disdéri, Paris, ca. 1865)

4

4. JENNY LIND (1820–1887), Swedish coloratura soprano. This legendary singer had already left the operatic stage before her enormously successful American tour sponsored by P. T. Barnum. 5. MARIETTA ALBONI (1823–1894), Italian contralto. She was one of the most highly acclaimed singers of the nineteenth century. 6. PASQUALE BRIGNOLI (1824–1884), Italian tenor. He was the most important tenor resident in the United States before the arrival of Jean de Reszke.

7. PAULINE VIARDOT-GARCÍA (1821–1910, of the celebrated García family of singers and teachers), French mezzo-soprano. A phenomenal singer, teacher and composer, she created the role of Fidès in Meyerbeer's *Le Prophète* and the title role in Gounod's *Sapho*. 8. MARIE MIOLAN-CARVALHO (1827–1895), French soprano, as Juliette in Gounod's *Roméo et Juliette*, a role she created (as well as Marguerite in his *Faust* and the title role in his *Mireille*).

5

6

7

8

9

10

9. JEAN-BAPTISTE FAURE (1830–1914), French baritone, in the title role of Thomas's *Hamlet*, which he created. A star of the Paris Opéra, where he also created the role of Nelusko in Meyerbeer's *L'Africaine*, Faure is the earliest-born great singer whose voice is preserved on records. 10. ALBERT NIEMANN (1831–1917), German tenor, as Tristan in Wagner's *Tristan und Isolde*. He created the role of Siegmund in *Die Walküre* and was the first Tristan and Siegfried (*Götterdämmerung*) in America. 11. (SIR) CHARLES SANTLEY (1834–1922), English baritone. Gounod composed the aria "Avant de quitter ces lieux" (*Faust*) especially for him. (Photo: Sarony, N.Y.) 12. THERESE TIETJENS (1831–1877), German soprano. Chiefly active in England, she also appeared at the Academy of Music in New York. (Photo: Elliott & Fry, London) 13 & 14. CARLOTTA MARCHISIO (1835–1872), Italian soprano, and BARBARA MARCHISIO (1833–1919), Italian contralto. Carlotta and Barbara Marchisio were sisters who gained great fame by their joint performances in such works as *Norma* and *Semiramide*.

11

12

13

14

6

26

25. ADELINA PATTI (1843–1919), coloratura soprano (born in Spain to Italian parents). Her career began in America while she was still a child. Eventually she was acclaimed as the greatest vocalist of her generation. (See also frontispiece.)
26. CHRISTINE (KRISTINA) NILSSON (1843–1921), Swedish coloratura soprano, possibly as Violetta in Verdi's *La Traviata.* Internationally hailed as the second "Swedish nightingale" (Jenny Lind being the first), she sang Marguerite at the opening of the Met in 1883. (Photo: Sarony, N.Y.)

27

28

27. AMALIE MATERNA (1844–1918), Austrian soprano, as Brünnhilde in Wagner's *Die Walküre.* A star of the Vienna Hofoper, she was the first Brünnhilde and Kundry (*Parsifal*) at Bayreuth. 28. ANGELO MASINI (1844–1926), Italian tenor. Verdi wrote the tenor role in the *Manzoni Requiem* for him. (Photo: Esplugas, Barcelona, ca. 1880)

29

30

29. ITALO CAMPANINI (1845–1896), Italian tenor. He sang the title role in Gounod's *Faust* at the opening night of the Met. His brother was the outstanding conductor Cleofonte Campanini. 30. EMMA THURSBY (1845–1931), American soprano. Her opera and concert career took her to the Far East as well as Europe and throughout the United States. (Photo: Falk, N.Y.)

31

31. MARIE RÔZE (1846–1926), French soprano, as Marguerite in Gounod's *Faust*. Highly successful in France and England, she was married for some time to the famous impresario James Henry Mapleson. (Photo: Mora, N.Y.) 32. EMMA ALBANI (Marie Lajeunesse, 1847–1930), Canadian soprano. Internationally famous, she was most closely associated with Covent Garden and was married to its impresario, Ernest Gye.

32

33

34

35

33. JEAN LASSALLE (1847–1909), French baritone, as Benvenuto Cellini in Saint-Saëns's *Ascanio*, a role he created. Other creations of his were Scindia in Massenet's *Le Roi de Lahore* and the title role in Saint-Saëns's *Henry VIII*. 34. JEAN LASSALLE as Nelusko in Meyerbeer's *L'Africaine*. 35. LUCIEN FUGÈRE (1848–1935), French baritone. A mainstay of the Opéra-Comique for decades, his many creations there included the Father in Charpentier's *Louise*. (Photo: Boyer & Bert, Paris)

16

37

38

36. LILLI LEHMANN (1848–1929), German soprano. One of the greatest phenomena in operatic history, for glory of voice, extent and variety of repertoire and length of career, she was also the guiding spirit of the Mozart festivals in Salzburg from 1901 to 1910; see also No. 65. (Photo: Falk, N.Y.). 37. VICTOR MAUREL (1848–1923), French baritone, in the title role of Verdi's *Falstaff*, which he created. This great singing actor was also the first Amonasro (Verdi's *Aïda*) in America, the original Iago in Verdi's *Otello* and the original Tonio in Leoncavallo's *I Pagliacci*. 38. VICTOR MAUREL in the title role of Mozart's *Don Giovanni*. (Photo: Dupont, N.Y.)

39

40

39. THEODOR REICHMANN (1849–1903), German baritone, as Hans Sachs in Wagner's *Die Meistersinger von Nürnberg*. This important singer, who appeared at the Met from 1889 to 1891, created the role of Amfortas in Wagner's *Parsifal*. 40. THEODOR REICHMANN as Amfortas. (Photo: Höffert, 1889) 41. JEAN DE RESZKE (Jan Mieczisław, 1850–1925, brother of Edouard and Josephine de Reszke), Polish tenor, as Roméo in Gounod's *Roméo et Juliette*. The greatest tenor of his generation, he created the title role in Massenet's *Le Cid* and became as renowned in Wagner as in the French and Italian repertoire. (Photo: Dupont, N.Y.)

41

42

43

44

42. GIUSEPPE KASCHMANN (1850–1925), Italian baritone. He sang in the first season of the Met. 43. SOFIA SCALCHI (1850–1922), Italian mezzo-soprano, as Frédéric in Thomas's *Mignon*. She was in the roster of the Met's first season. (Photo: Mora, N.Y.) 44. MINNIE HAUK (Mignon Hauck, 1851–1929), American soprano, as Marguerite in Gounod's *Faust*. She was the first American Juliette, Manon and Carmen (her greatest role). (Photo: Mora, N.Y.) 45. FRANCESCO TAMAGNO (1850–1905), Italian heroic tenor, in the title role of Verdi's *Otello*, which he created.

45

48

46

47

46. EDOUARD DE RESZKE (Edouard Mieczisław, 1853–1917, brother of Jean and Josephine de Reszke), Polish bass. He was the leading bass of the Paris Opéra from 1885 to 1898 and sang at the Met from 1891 to 1903. (Photo: Dupont, N.Y.) 47. EDOUARD DE RESZKE as Méphistophélès in Gounod's *Faust*. 48. JOSEPHINE DE RESZKE (Josephine Mieczisław, 1855–1891, sister of Jean and Edouard de Reszke), Polish soprano. She sang at the Paris Opéra and in Madrid and Lisbon.

50

49

49. POL (PAUL-HENRI) PLANÇON (1854–1914), French bass, as Saint-Bris in Meyerbeer's *Les Huguenots.* Possessor of a trill said to be the envy of many a soprano, he was the leading bass at the Met between 1893 and 1908. (Photo: Dupont, N.Y.) 50. POL PLANÇON. (Photo: Falk, N.Y., autographed 1894)

24

52

53

51. ETELKA GERSTER (1855–1920), Hungarian soprano, as Amina in Bellini's *La Sonnambula*. She enjoyed an international reputation as a prima donna assoluta. (Photo: Mora, N.Y.) 52. MATTIA BATTISTINI (1856–1928), Italian baritone, as Prince Yeletsky in Tchaikovsky's *Pikovaya Dama* (Queen of Spades). "King of baritones" of his day, he was one of the supreme recording artists. 53. MATTIA BATTISTINI in the title role of Verdi's *Rigoletto*.

55

54

56

57

58

54. DAVID BISPHAM (1857–1921), American baritone. He enjoyed a successful career at Covent Garden and the Met and sang in oratorio. (Photo: Hartsook, Los Angeles, 1914). 55. NIKOLAI FIGNER (1856–1919), Russian tenor, as Raoul in Meyerbeer's *Les Huguenots*. He created the role of Herman in Tchaikovsky's *Pikovaya Dama* (Queen of Spades), as well as other important tenor roles by Tchaikovsky, Napravnik and Catalani. 56. BEN DAVIES (1858–1943), Welsh tenor. He created the title role in Sir Arthur Sullivan's *Ivanhoe* and concertized extensively. 57. LILLIAN NORDICA (Lillian Norton, 1857–1914), American soprano, as Isolde in Wagner's *Tristan und Isolde*. Internationally famous, she was a Met attraction from 1891 to 1909 and also sang with the Manhattan and Boston companies. 58. LILLIAN NORDICA in the title role of Verdi's *Aïda*. (Photo: Dupont, N.Y.)

59

60

61

62

63

64

59. EMMA CALVÉ (1858–1942), French soprano, in the title role of Bizet's *Carmen* (card scene), her most famous characterization. During her fabulous worldwide career, she created the roles of Susel in Mascagni's *L'Amico Fritz,* Anita in Massenet's *La Navarraise* and the title role of the same composer's *Sapho.* (Photo: Falk, N.Y., 1893) 60. EMMA CALVÉ as Santuzza in Mascagni's *Cavalleria rusticana.* 61. EMMA CALVÉ as Ophélie in Thomas's *Hamlet.* (Photo: Reutlinger) 62. EMMA CALVÉ as Carmen. 63. MARCELLA SEMBRICH (Praxede Kochańska, 1858–1935), Polish coloratura soprano (born in then-Austrian Galicia), as Rosina in Rossini's *Il Barbiere di Siviglia.* At the Met in 1883 and from 1898 to 1909, this superb singer later taught in Berlin, Lausanne, Philadelphia (Curtis Institute) and New York (Juilliard). (Photo: Dupont, N.Y.) 64. MARCELLA SEMBRICH.

65

66

65. FRANCISCO D'ANDRADE (1859–1921), Portuguese baritone, in his most famous part, the title role of Mozart's *Don Giovanni*, with Lilli Lehmann (see No. 36) as Donna Anna. D'Andrade enjoyed international fame. 66. LÉON ESCALAÏS (1859–1941), French heroic tenor. His brilliant voice was often heard in Paris, Brussels and Milan.

67

68

67. MARIO ANCONA (1860–1931), Italian baritone. He created the role of Silvio in Leoncavallo's *I Pagliacci.* During his worldwide career, he sang at the Met, the Manhattan Opera House, the Boston Opera and the Chicago Opera. (Photo: Falk, N.Y.) 68. FERNANDO DE LUCIA (1860–1925), Italian tenor. Among the roles created by this celebrated singer were Fritz Kobus in Mascagni's *L'Amico Fritz* and Osaka in the same composer's *Iris.* (Photo: Marvuglia, Naples, inscribed to Barbara Marchisio—see No. 14—and dated 1896)

69

70

69. FELIA LITVINNE (1860–1936), Russian soprano, as Isolde in Wagner's *Tristan und Isolde*. Chiefly active in Paris, she appeared at the Met in the 1896/1897 season. 70. EUGENIA MANTELLI (1860–1926), Italian mezzo-soprano, as the Prologue in Mancinelli's *Ero e Leandro*. She sang at the Met between 1894 and 1903.

71

72

71. SIGRID ARNOLDSON (1861–1943), Swedish coloratura soprano, as Juliette in Gounod's *Roméo et Juliette*. This third "Swedish nightingale" had a great international career. 72. ZÉLIE DE LUSSAN (1861–1949), American mezzo-soprano, in the title role of Bizet's *Carmen*, her most famous part. She was at the Met between 1894 and 1900, at Covent Garden from 1895 to 1902.

73

74

73. (DAME) NELLIE MELBA (Helen Mitchell, 1861–1931), Australian soprano, as Ophélie in Thomas's *Hamlet*. One of the very greatest turn-of-the-century singers, she performed all over the world, reigning as undisputed queen at Covent Garden. 74. NELLIE MELBA, probably as Juliette in Gounod's *Roméo et Juliette*. 75. NELLIE MELBA as Marguerite in Gounod's *Faust*. (Photo: Dupont, N.Y., 1896)

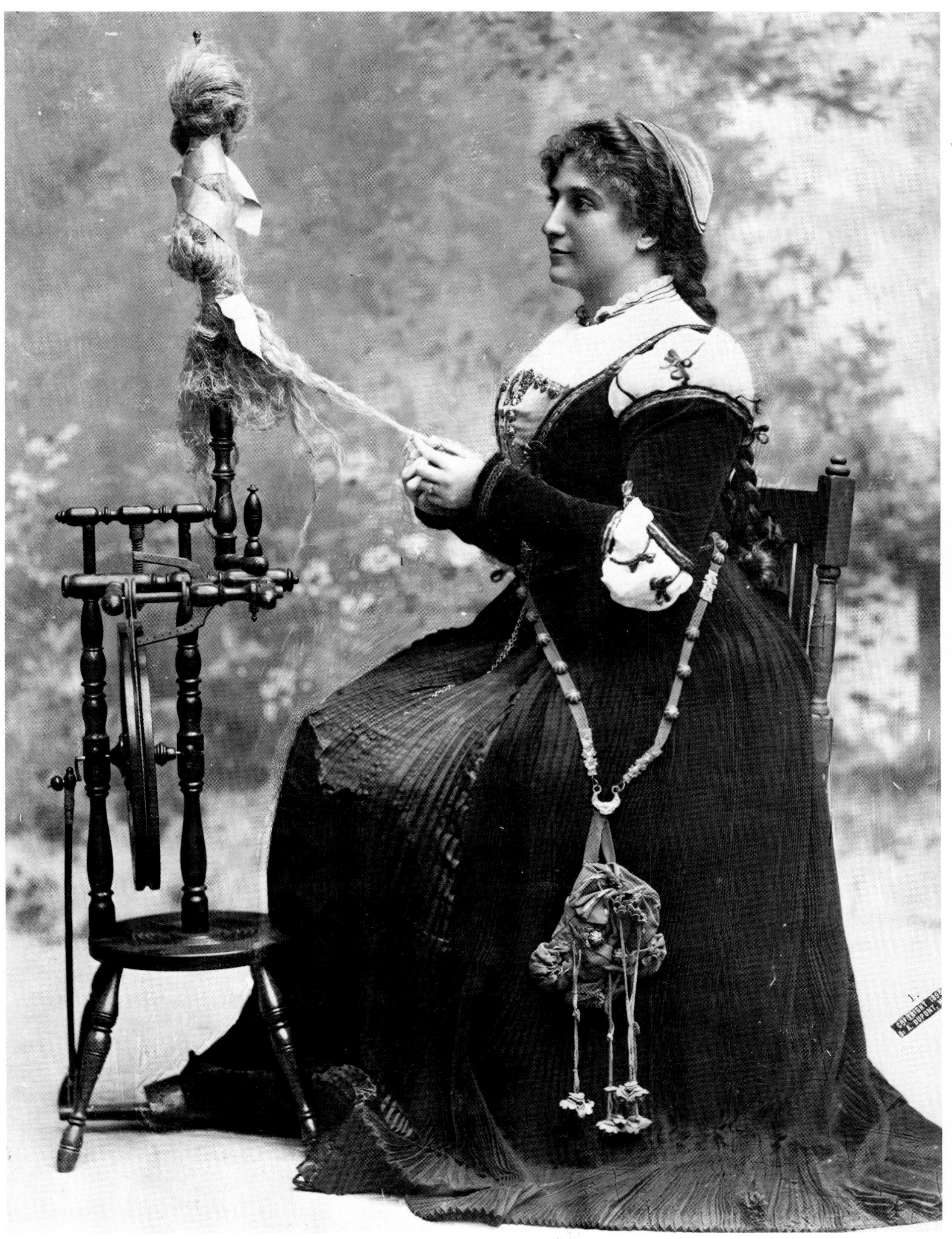

75

77

76. MAURICE RENAUD (1861–1933), French baritone, probably as Hérode in Massenet's *Hérodiade*. Among the roles he created were the High Priest in Reyer's *Sigurd* and Boniface in Massenet's *Le Jongleur de Notre-Dame*. In America he performed at the Manhattan Opera House, the Met, Chicago and Boston. 77. ERNEST VAN DYCK (1861–1923), Belgian tenor. This outstanding Wagnerian singer also created the title role of Massenet's *Werther*. (Photo: Dupont, N.Y., autographed 1899)

78

79

78. ERNESTINE SCHUMANN-HEINK (1861–1936), German contralto (born near Prague), as Magdalene in Wagner's *Die Meistersinger von Nürnberg*, with Johanna Gadski (see No. 109) as Eva. The most important contralto of her day, at the Met from 1899 to 1932, Schumann-Heink created the role of Klytämnestra in Strauss's *Elektra* (see No. 150). 79. ERNESTINE SCHUMANN-HEINK in the American operetta *Love's Lottery* (by Julian Edwards, 1904). (Photo: Dupont, N.Y.)

80

81

82

80. ELLEN GULBRANSON (1863–1947), Swedish soprano, as Brünnhilde in Wagner's *Die Walküre*. She was chiefly associated with Bayreuth, where she appeared regularly from 1896 to 1914. 81. EMMA JUCH (1863–1939), American soprano (born Vienna), as Marguerite in Gounod's *Faust*. She is perhaps best remembered as the director of her own itinerant opera company in the United States from 1888 to 1891. 82. MILKA TERNINA (1863–1941), Croatian soprano, as Kundry in Wagner's *Parsifal*. Best known as a Wagnerian, she was the first Tosca as well as the first Kundry at the Met. 83. MILKA TERNINA as Brünnhilde in Wagner's *Die Walküre*.

83

84

85

84. GEMMA BELLINCIONI (1864–1950), Italian soprano. The principal female interpreter of *verismo*, she created the role of Santuzza in Mascagni's *Cavalleria rusticana* and the title role of Giordano's *Fedora*. (Photo: Bernoud) 85. FRANCESCO VIGNAS (Francisco Viñas, 1863–1933), Spanish heroic tenor, as Radames in Verdi's *Aïda*. At the Met from 1893 to 1897, he was the first Turiddu in America.

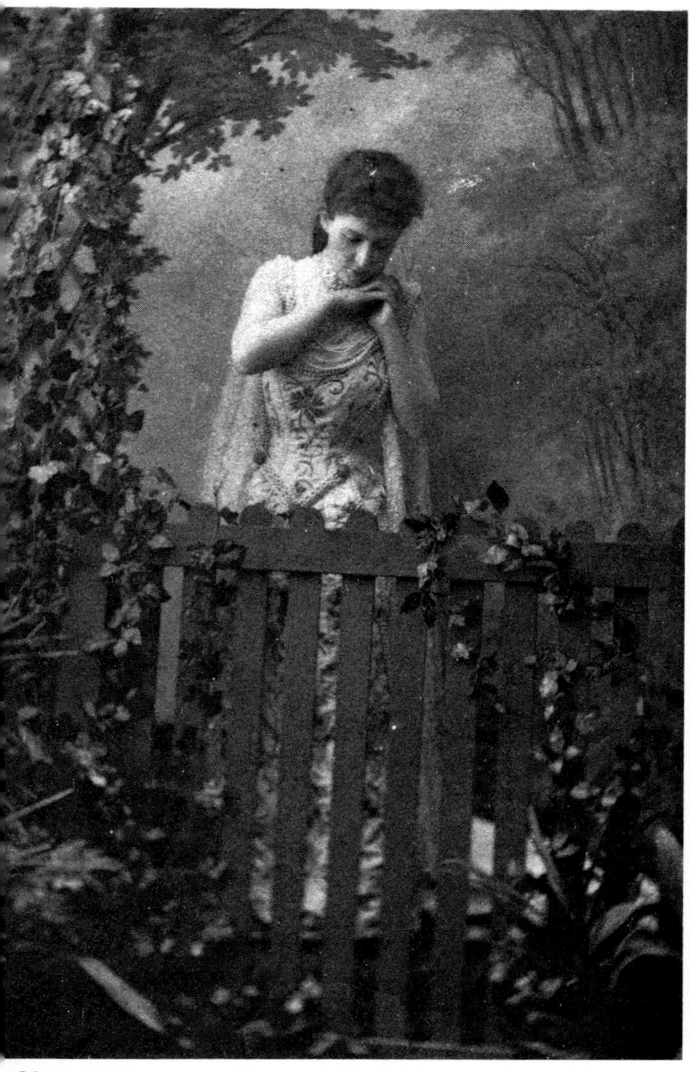

86

87

88

EMMA EAMES (1865–1952), American soprano (born ghai), as Juliette in Gounod's *Roméo et Juliette*. This was début role at the Paris Opéra in 1889, the year of this photo ographed and dated on the mounting). Juliette was also début role at the Met in 1891; she remained there until 1909 ne of the very great stars. 87. EMMA EAMES. 88. EMMA MES as Amelia in Verdi's *Un Ballo in maschera*.

Paul Knüpfer
als Pogner in „Die Meistersinger v. Nürnberg."
Kunstverlag Emil Schwalb
Berlin-Charlottenburg 4.
1348

89

90

89. PAUL KNÜPFER (1865–1920), German bass, as Pogner in Wagner's *Die Meistersinger von Nürnberg*. Knüpfer was a leading member of the Berlin Opera. 90. HENRI ALBERS (1866–1925), Dutch baritone, as the Father in Charpentier's *Louise*. He was with the Opéra-Comique from 1899 until his death. 91. SIBYL SANDERSON (1865–1903), American soprano, in the title role of Massenet's *Thaïs*, which she created, as well as the title roles of the same composer's *Esclarmonde* and Saint-Saëns's *Phryné*.

91

92

92. ANTONIO SCOTTI (1886–1936), Italian baritone. First baritone at the Met for 34 years, for a time director of his own traveling company, he created the role of Chim-Fen in Leoni's *L'Oracolo*. 93. LUCIENNE BRÉVAL (Bertha Schilling, 1869–1935), Swiss soprano (born Berlin), in the title role of Reyer's *Salammbô*. A member of the Paris Opéra for over 25 years, she created the title roles of Massenet's *Grisélidis*, Février's *Monna Vanna* and Fauré's *Pénélope*. 94. CHARLES GILIBERT (1866–1910), French baritone. This well-liked singer appeared at the Met and the Manhattan Opera House. (Photo: Dupont, N.Y.) 95. EDMOND CLÉMENT (1867–1928), French tenor, as Don José in Bizet's *Carmen*. The outstanding French lyric tenor of his generation, he sang at the Met and in Boston. 96. EDMOND CLÉMENT as Rodolfo in Puccini's *La Bohème*. (Photo: Nadar)

93

94

95

96

97

97. MARCEL JOURNET (1867–1933), French bass, as Méphistophélès in Gounod's *Faust*, his greatest role. One of the leading twentieth-century basses, he created the role of Simon Mago in Boito's *Nerone*. (Photo: Dupont, N.Y.)

98

98. JOSÉ MARDONES (1869–1932), Spanish bass, as Ramfis in Verdi's *Aïda*. After a long career in Europe and South America, he was with the Boston Opera from 1913 to 1916 and at the Met from 1917 to 1926. (Photo: Mishkin, N.Y.)

99

100

101

102

99. ANTON VAN ROOY (1870–1932), Dutch baritone, as Wotan in Wagner's *Das Rheingold* or *Die Walküre*. This outstanding singer was the first Amfortas (*Parsifal*) and Jokanaan (*Salome*) at the Met. (Photo: Dupont, N.Y., 1898) 100. CHARLES DALMORÈS (1871–1939), French tenor. Internationally active (including the Manhattan Opera House and the Chicago Opera), he created the role of Win-San-Luy in Leoni's *L'Oracolo*. 101. HEINRICH KNOTE (1870–1953), German heroic tenor, in the title role of Verdi's *Otello*. He was at the met from 1904 to 1908. 102. ALESSANDRO BONCI (1870–1940), Italian tenor. This lyrical master of bel canto, considered Caruso's chief rival, sang at the Manhattan Opera House and the Met, and in Europe and South America.

52

104

103. OLIVE FREMSTAD (1871–1951), American soprano (born Stockholm), as Isolde in Wagner's *Tristan und Isolde.* At the Met from 1903 to 1914, she was the first Salome (Strauss) in America. (Photo: Mishkin, N.Y.) 104. EUGENIO GIRALDONI (1871–1924), Italian baritone (born Marseilles). He created the role of Scarpia in Puccini's *La Tosca.* (Photo: Klar, Tiflis)

105

106

105. LOUISE HOMER (1871–1947), American contralto, as Amneris in Verdi's *Aïda*. One of the greatest contraltos of her time, she sang at the Met 1900–1919 and 1927–1930, at the Chicago Opera 1920–1925. She created the role of the Witch in Humperdinck's *Königskinder*. (Photo: Dupont, N.Y., 1909) 106. LOUISE HOMER as Lola in Mascagni's *Cavalleria rusticana*. (Photo: Dupont, N.Y.)

107

108

107 & 108. LUISA TETRAZZINI (1871–1940), Italian coloratura soprano. Outstanding attraction of the Manhattan Opera House, the Met and the Chicago Opera, she was considered by many as a well-nigh perfect coloratura.

109

110

109. JOHANNA GADSKI (1872–1932), German soprano, as Pamina in Mozart's *Die Zauberflöte*. She was a star of the Met from 1900 to 1917. (Photo: Dupont, N.Y.) 110. JOHANNA GADSKI as Brünnhilde in Wagner's *Die Walküre*. (Photo: Dupont, N.Y.) See also No. 78.

111

112

111. FRIEDRICH WEIDEMANN (1871–1919), German baritone, probably as Hans Sachs in Wagner's *Die Meistersinger von Nürnberg.* He was a member of the Vienna Opera from 1903 until his death. (Photo: Angerer, Vienna) 112. ANNA BAHR-MILDENBURG (1872–1947), Austrian soprano, as Ortrud in Wagner's *Lohengrin.* She starred at the Vienna Opera from 1898 to 1917, excelling in Wagnerian roles, and was later the teacher of Lauritz Melchior.

113

114

113. ENRICO CARUSO (1873–1921), Italian tenor, as Don José in Bizet's *Carmen.* The most popular of all opera singers on stage and on records, Caruso created such important roles as Loris Ipanov in Giordano's *Fedora,* Conte Maurizio in Cilèa's *Adriana Lecouvreur,* Federico Loewe in Franchetti's *Germania* and Dick Johnson in Puccini's *La Fanciulla del West.* (Photo: Dupont, N.Y.) 114. ENRICO CARUSO as Samson in Saint-Saëns's *Samson et Dalila.* (Photo: Mishkin, N.Y.)

115

116

117

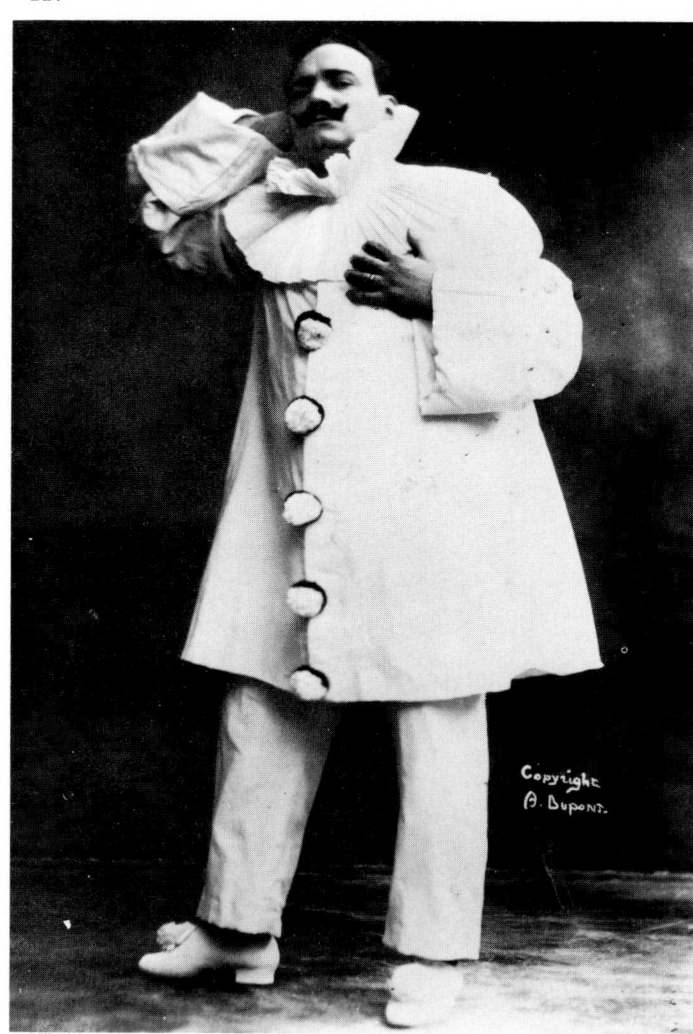

118

ENRICO CARUSO. 115. As Radames in Verdi's *Aïda.* (Photo: Mishkin, N.Y.) 116. In private life. 117. As Lionel in Flotow's *Martha.* (Photo: Dupont, N.Y.). 118. As Canio in Leoncavallo's *I Pagliacci.* (Photo: Dupont, N.Y.)

119

120

121

122

123

124

119. OTTO GORITZ (1873–1929), German baritone, as the Fiddler in Humperdinck's *Königskinder*, a role he created. At the Met from 1903 to 1917, he was also the first Baron von Ochs (*Rosenkavalier*) in America. 120. OTTO GORITZ as Werner Kirchhofer in Nessler's *Der Trompeter von Säkkingen*. 121. ANDREA (ANDRÉS) DE SEGUROLA (1873–1953), Spanish bass. He sang at the Manhattan Opera House and the Met, where he was the original Jake Wallace in Puccini's *La Fanciulla del West* and Nicolao in the same composer's *Gianni Schicchi*. (Photo: Mishkin, N.Y.) 122. LOUISE KIRKBY-LUNN (1873–1930), English contralto. She sang at Covent Garden and the Met. 123. MARIE RAPPOLD (1853–1957), soprano (born in London to German parents), as Helen of Troy in Boito's *Mefistofele*. She was on the Met roster between 1905 and 1920. (Photo: Dupont, N.Y.) 124. MARIE RAPPOLD as Leonora in Verdi's *Il Trovatore*. (Photo: Elzin, N.Y.) See also No. 141.

125

126

125. FEODOR CHALIAPIN (1873–1938), Russian bass, in the title role of Massenet's *Don Quichotte*, which he created. One of the supreme singing actors, he enjoyed an international career of matchless success. 126. MARIO SAMMARCO (1873–1930), Italian baritone, as Scarpia in Puccini's *La Tosca*. He created the roles of Gérard in Giordano's *Andrea Chenier*, Cascart in Leoncavallo's *Zazà* and Carlo Worms in Franchetti's *Germania*. (Photo: Matzene, Chicago)

127

128

127. LEO SLEZAK (1873–1946), Moravian heroic tenor. A brilliant star of the Vienna Opera from 1901 to 1926, he appeared at the Met 1909–1912. (Photo: Zander & Labisch) 128. LEO SLEZAK in the title role of Verdi's *Otello*.

129

130

129. HERBERT WITHERSPOON (1873–1935), American bass, as Méphistophélès in Gounod's *Faust*. At the Met from 1908 to 1916, he was later director of the Chicago Opera. He was appointed director of the Met in 1935 but died shortly thereafter and was replaced by Edward Johnson. (Photo: Dupont, N.Y.)
130. HERBERT WITHERSPOON as Landgrave Hermann in Wagner's *Tannhäuser*. (Photo: Dupont, N.Y.)

131

132

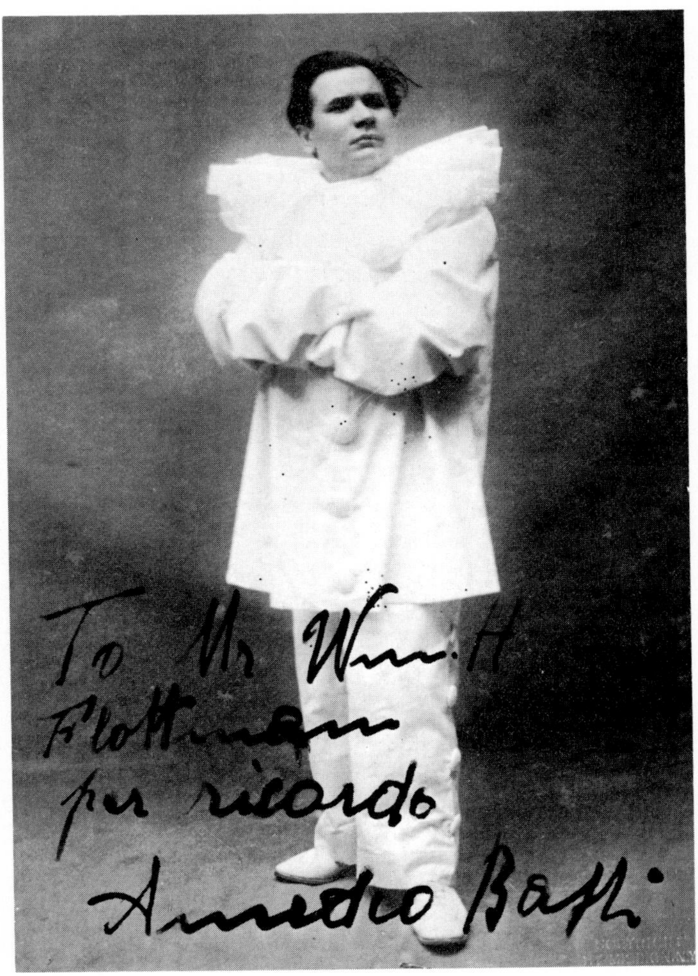

133

131. KARL JÖRN (1873–1947), German tenor (born Riga), in the title role of Gounod's *Faust*. He was a star of the Berlin Opera and the Met. (Photo: Dupont, N.Y., 1909) 132. AMEDEO BASSI (1874–1949), Italian tenor, as Gennaro in Wolf-Ferrari's *I Gioielli della Madonna*. He sang at the Manhattan Opera House, the Met and the Chicago Opera. (Photo: Matzene, Chicago) 133. AMEDEO BASSI as Canio in Leoncavallo's *I Pagliacci*. (Photo: Mishkin, N.Y.)

134

135

136

134. MARIE GUTHEIL-SCHODER (1874–1935), German soprano, as Gutrune in Wagner's *Die Götterdämmerung*. She was with the Vienna Opera from 1900 to 1926. 135. LINA CAVALIERI (1874–1944), Italian soprano, as Nedda in Leoncavallo's *I Pagliacci*. Remembered more for her beauty than her vocal achievements, she nevertheless had a remarkable operatic career. 136. EMILIO DE GOGORZA (1874–1949), baritone (born in Brooklyn to Spanish parents). A popular concert and recording artist who never appeared on the operatic stage, he became artistic director of the Victor Company. For some years he was married to Emma Eames (see No. 86). (Photo: Dupont, N.Y., autographed 1898)

137

138

137 & 138. MARY GARDEN (1874–1967), Scottish soprano, in two aspects of the title role of Strauss's *Salome*. Among her numerous creations was the role of Mélisande in Debussy's *Pelléas et Mélisande*. She was at the Manhattan Opera House from 1907 to 1910, and the top star of the Chicago Opera from 1910 to 1930. (Photo 138: Mishkin, N.Y.)

139

140

141

139. SELMA KURZ (1874–1933), Austrian coloratura soprano (born Galicia). A sensation of the Vienna Opera from 1899 to 1929, she was acclaimed throughout Europe. 140. RICCARDO MARTIN (Hugh Whitfield Martin, 1874–1952), American tenor. He sang at the Met, Boston Opera and Chicago Opera, and was the original Christian in Damrosch's *Cyrano de Bergerac.* (Photo: Dupont, N.Y.) 141. RICCARDO MARTIN in the title role of Gounod's *Faust*, with Marie Rappold (see No. 123) as Marguerite. (Photo: Dupont, N.Y.)

142

143

144

142. ADAMO DIDUR (1874–1946), Polish bass (born Galicia), in the title role of Mussorgsky's *Boris Godunov*, with ANNA CASE (born 1889), American soprano, as Fyodor. This was the first production of the opera in America (1913). Didur was at the Met from 1907 to 1933. Case, at the Met between 1909 and 1920, was the first Sophie (*Rosenkavalier*) in the United States. (Photo: White, N.Y.) 143. RICCARDO STRACCIARI (1875–1955), Italian baritone, in the title role of Verdi's *Rigoletto*. He sang at the Met and the Chicago Opera as well as in Europe and South America. 144. PAUL BENDER (1875–1947), German bass, as Fasolt in Wagner's *Das Rheingold*. First bass of the Munich Opera from 1903 to 1933, he appeared at the Met 1922–1927. (Photo: A. Baumann)

145

146

147

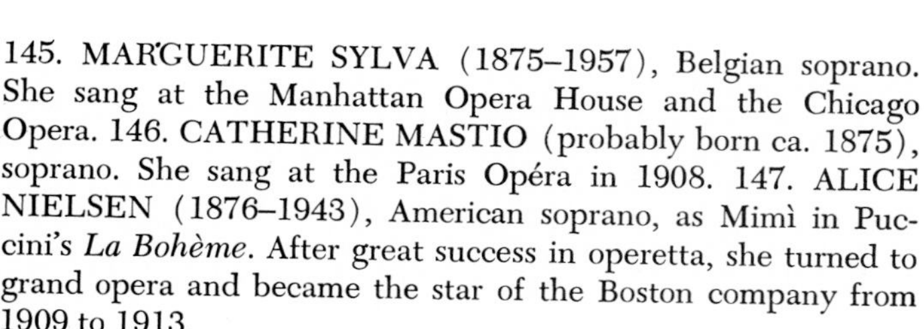

145. MARGUERITE SYLVA (1875–1957), Belgian soprano. She sang at the Manhattan Opera House and the Chicago Opera. 146. CATHERINE MASTIO (probably born ca. 1875), soprano. She sang at the Paris Opéra in 1908. 147. ALICE NIELSEN (1876–1943), American soprano, as Mimì in Puccini's *La Bohème*. After great success in operetta, she turned to grand opera and became the star of the Boston company from 1909 to 1913.

148

149

148 & 149. GIUSEPPE DE LUCA (1876–1950), Italian baritone. Among his creations were Sharpless in the original version of Puccini's *Madama Butterfly*, Paquiro in Granados' *Goyescas* and the title role of Puccini's *Gianni Schicchi*. He was one of the most distinguished baritones at the Met from 1915 to 1946. (Photo 149: A. Ermini, Milan) See also No. 186.

150

151

152

150. ANNIE KRULL (1876–1947), German soprano, in the title role of Strauss's *Elektra,* which she created, with Ernestine Schumann-Heink (see No. 78) as Klytämnestra. Krull also created the roles of Diemuth in Strauss's *Feuersnot* and Ulana in Paderewski's *Manru.* 151. GIOVANNI ZENATELLO (1876–1949), Italian tenor. The original Pinkerton in Puccini's *Madama Butterfly,* he was also considered the best Otello after Tamagno. He appeared at the Manhattan Opera House, Boston and Chicago. (Photo: A. Ermini, Milan) 152. GIOVANNI ZENATELLO as Dick Johnson in Puccini's *La Fanciulla del West.*

153

154

155

156

157

153. NICOLA ZEROLA (1876–1936), Italian tenor. He sang at the Manhattan Opera House and in Chicago. (Photo: Emile Bauwens). 154. EMMA CARELLI (1877–1928), Italian soprano, in the title role of Puccini's *La Tosca*. An important *verismo* singer, she was director of the Teatro Costanzi in Rome from 1910 to 1926. (Photo: F. Felicetti, Rome) 155. RICHARD MAYR (1877–1935), Austrian bass. Star of the Vienna Opera from 1902 until his death, he was a celebrated Ochs in *Der Rosenkavalier* and created the role of Barak in Strauss's *Die Frau ohne Schatten*. 156. RICHARD MAYR as King Heinrich in Wagner's *Lohengrin*. 157. HERMANN JADLOWKER (1877–1953), German tenor (born Riga), as Walther von Stolzing in Wagner's *Die Meistersinger von Nürnberg*. This outstanding singer created the roles of the King's Son in Humperdinck's *Königskinder* and Bacchus in Strauss's *Ariadne auf Naxos*. He possessed an extraordinary technique (including a phenomenal trill), which allowed him to excel in such diverse roles as Parsifal and Don Ottavio. (Photo: E. Bieber, Berlin)

158

159

158. TITTA RUFFO (Ruffo Cafiero Titta, 1877–1953), Italian baritone, as he looked upon his arrival in America in 1912 to join the Chicago Opera. This exceptional singer was at the Met from 1921 to 1929. 159. TITTA RUFFO as Neri Chiaramantesi in Giordano's *La Cena delle beffe*. 160. TITTA RUFFO in the title role of Verdi's *Rigoletto*. (Photo: Matzene, Chicago)

160

161

162

161. CELESTINA BONINSEGNA (1877–1947), Italian soprano, as Helen of Troy in Boito's *Mefistofele*. This great recording artist had a wandering career that took her to many parts of the world. 162. (JEAN-EMILE) VANNI-MARCOUX (1877–1962), bass-baritone (born in Turin to French parents) as the Father in Charpentier's *Louise*. He sang at Boston and Chicago and directed the Bordeaux Opera from 1948 to 1952. (Photo: Dover St. Studios, London)

163

164

163. BESSIE ABOTT (Bessie Pickens, 1878–1919), American soprano, as Marguerite in Gounod's *Faust*. She sang at the Met from 1906 to 1909. (Photo: Dupont, N.Y.) 164. BESSIE ABOTT as Elisabeth in Wagner's *Tannhäuser*. (Photo: Reutlinger)

165

166

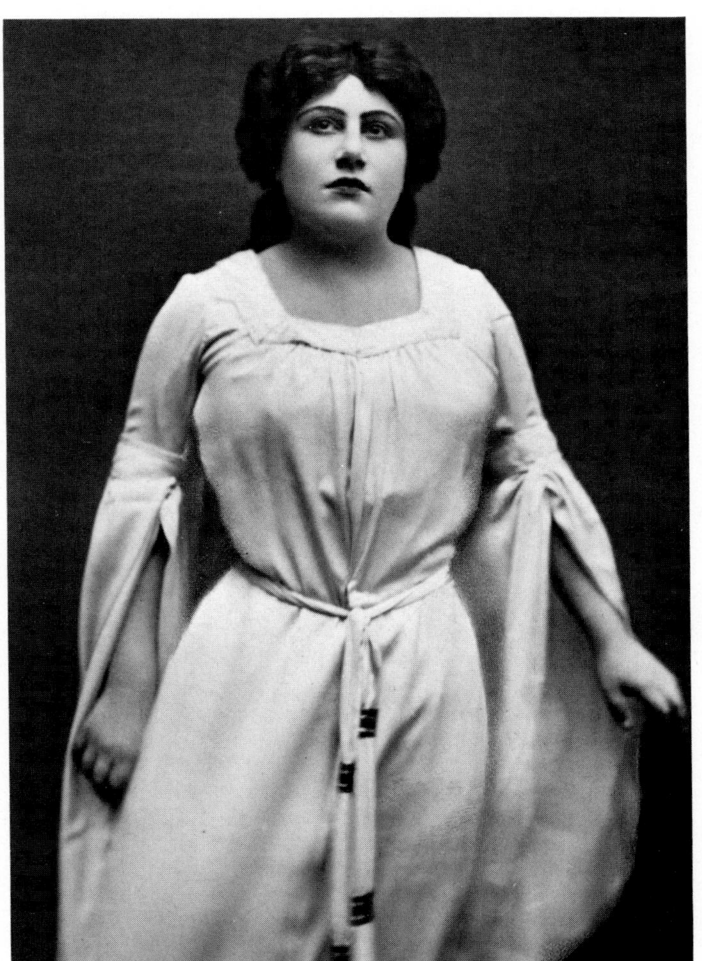

167

165. PASQUALE AMATO (1878–1942), Italian baritone, as Scarpia in Puccini's *La Tosca.* This brilliant singer created the roles of Jack Rance in Puccini's *La Fanciulla del West,* Napoleon in Giordano's *Madame Sans-Gêne* and the title role of Damrosch's *Cyrano de Bergerac.* (Photo: Mishkin, N.Y.) 166. EMMY DESTINN (Emmy Kittl, 1878–1930), Bohemian soprano, as Queen Marguerite in Meyerbeer's *Les Huguenots.* At the Met between 1908 and 1921, this great singer created the role of Minnie in Puccini's *La Fanciulla del West.* (Photo: Mishkin, N.Y.) 167. EMMY DESTINN as Elsa in Wagner's *Lohengrin.*

168

169

170

171

172

173

168. ELEONORA DE CISNEROS (1878–1934), American mezzo-soprano, as Amneris in Verdi's *Aïda*. She was a star of the Manhattan Opera House and the Chicago Opera. (Photo: Mishkin, N.Y.) 169. MARÍA GAY (1879–1943), Spanish mezzo-soprano, in the title role of Bizet's *Carmen*. She sang at the Met, Boston and Chicago. She was married to the tenor Giovanni Zenatello (see No. 151). 170. EMMA TRENTINI (1878–1959), Italian soprano, as Musetta in Puccini's *La Bohème*, her best role at the Manhattan Opera House. She is chiefly remembered today for her subsequent operetta creations in Herbert's *Naughty Marietta* and Friml's *The Firefly*. (Photo: Mishkin, N.Y., 1906) 171. EDWARD JOHNSON (1878–1959), Canadian tenor. With the Chicago Opera 1919–1922 and the Met 1922–1935, he directed the latter company from 1935 to 1950. He created the roles of Aethelwold in Taylor's *The King's Henchman*, the title role of the same composer's *Peter Ibbetson* and Sir Gower Lackland in Hanson's *Merry Mount*. (Photo: Mishkin, N.Y.) 172. ARISTODEMO GIORGINI (1879–1937), Italian tenor, as Rodolfo in Puccini's *La Bohème*. He sang in Chicago and throughout Europe, specializing in Bellini and other Italian composers. (Photo: Matzene, Chicago) 173. ARISTODEMO GIORGINI in private life. (Photo: Matzene, Chicago)

174

175

174. FRITZI SCHEFF (1879–1954), Austrian soprano. At the Met 1900–1904, she then turned to operetta, gaining her principal fame in Herbert's *Mlle. Modiste*.
175. LUCIE WEIDT (1879–1940), German soprano (born Bohemia), probably as Elisabeth in Wagner's *Tannhäuser*. At the Vienna Opera from 1903 to 1926, she created the role of the Nurse in Strauss's *Die Frau ohne Schatten*. (Photo: Pietzner, Vienna)

176

177

176 & 177. MARGARET(HE) MATZENAUER (1881–1963), mezzo-soprano (born Temesvár). She sang at the Met from 1911 to 1930. (Photos: 176, Mishkin, N.Y.; 177: Apeda, N.Y.)

183

184

185

186

GERALDINE FARRAR. 183. In the title role of Massenet's *Thaïs*. 184. As Rosaura in Wolf-Ferrari's *Le Donne curiose*. 185. As Marguerite in Gounod's *Faust*. 186. As Cherubino in Mozart's *Le Nozze di Figaro*, with Giuseppe de Luca (see No. 148) as Figaro. (Photo: White, N.Y.)

187

187. AMELITA GALLI-CURCI (1882–1963), Italian coloratura soprano, in the title role of Delibes's *Lakmé*. After her great success in Chicago 1916–1918, she sang at the Met 1921–1931, becoming the most famous coloratura of the century. (Photo: Matzene, Chicago)

188

188. DIMITRI SMIRNOV (1882–1944), Russian tenor, as Roméo in Gounod's *Roméo et Juliette*. He was the most important Russian tenor of his generation. (Photo: Fisher)

189

190

191

192

193

194

189. CARLO GALEFFI (1882–1961), Italian baritone. He created the roles of Manfredo in Montemezzi's *L'Amore dei tre Rè* and Fanuel in Boito's *Nerone*. 190. HELENE WILDBRUNN (born 1882), Austrian soprano, as Isolde in Wagner's *Tristan und Isolde*. She was chiefly associated with the Berlin and Vienna Operas. 191. GEORGETTE LEBLANC (born 1882), Belgian soprano. Mistress of the playwright Maeterlinck, she also acted in his works. 192. GEORGETTE LEBLANC in the title role of Massenet's *Thaïs*. (Photo: Dupont, Brussels) 193. FRANCES ALDA (Frances Davies, 1883–1952), New Zealand soprano. Wife of Met director Gatti-Casazza, she sang there 1908–1930, creating the role of Roxane in Damrosch's *Cyrano de Bergerac*. 194. FRANCES ALDA in the title role of Catalani's *La Wally*. (Photo: Dupont, N.Y.)

195

196

197

198

199

200

195. EDWARD LANKOW (Edward Rosenberg, 1883–1940), American bass. He sang at Boston, the Met and Chicago. (Photo: Mishkin, N.Y.) 196. NANNY LARSÉN-TODSEN (born 1884), Swedish soprano, as Isolde in Wagner's *Tristan und Isolde*. She specialized in Wagnerian roles. 197. GIUSEPPE DANISE (1883–1963), Italian baritone, in the title role of Rossini's *Guillaume Tell*. He was at the Met 1920–1932, and later married the soprano Bidú Sayão (see No. 305). (Photo: White, N.Y.) 198. ARMAND CRABBÉ (1883–1947), Belgian baritone, probably in the title role of Thomas's *Hamlet*. He enjoyed an international career. 199. FLORENCE EASTON (1884–1955), English soprano, as Fiordiligi in Mozart's *Così fan tutte*. From 1917 to 1929 she was at the Met, where she created the roles of Lauretta in Puccini's *Gianni Schicchi* and Aelfrida in Taylor's *The King's Henchman*. (Photo: Mishkin, N.Y.) 200. MARÍA BARRIENTOS (1883–1946), Spanish coloratura soprano. Her worldwide career included five seasons at the Met, 1915–1920. (Photo: Mishkin, N.Y.)

201

201. ALMA GLUCK (Reba Fiersohn, 1884–1938), American soprano (born Bucharest), as Micaëla in Bizet's *Carmen*. She sang at the Met 1909–1918 and was married to the violin virtuoso Efrem Zimbalist. (Photo: Mishkin, N.Y.) 202. JOHN McCORMACK (1884–1945), Irish tenor, in the title role of Gounod's *Faust*. One of the outstanding twentieth-century opera and concert singers, he is also one of the great names in the history of recordings.

202

203

204

205

203. ALICE ZEPPILLI (born 1884), coloratura soprano. She sang at the Manhattan Opera House and the Chicago Opera. (Photo: Mishkin, N.Y.) 204. MARGARETHE (ARNDT-) OBER (born 1885), German mezzo-soprano, as Dalila in Saint-Saëns's *Samson et Dalila.* She was at the met 1913–1916. 205. CARMEN MELIS (1885–1967), Italian soprano, as Sélika in Meyerbeer's *L'Africaine.* She appeared at the Manhattan Opera House and in Boston, but her greatest successes came later in Italy. 206. AURELIANO PERTILE (1885–1952), Italian tenor, as Edgardo in Donizetti's *Lucia di Lammermoor.* First tenor at La Scala from 1922 to 1940, he was a favorite singer of Toscanini's and created the title roles in Boito's *Nerone* and Wolf-Ferrari's *Sly.* (Photo: M. Castagneri)

206

207

208

207. FRIEDA HEMPEL (1885–1955), German coloratura soprano. This eminent singer was at the Met 1912–1920 and was the first Marschallin (*Rosenkavalier*) in America. (Photo: Ernst Schneider) 208. FRIEDA HEMPEL as Rosina in Rossini's *Il Barbiere di Siviglia.* (Photo: Mishkin, N.Y.) 209. FRIEDA HEMPEL as Gilda in Verdi's *Rigoletto.*

209

210

211

210. GIOVANNI MARTINELLI (1885–1969), Italian tenor, in the title role of Verdi's *Otello.* He was one of the principal tenors of the Met from 1913 to 1946, creating the roles of Lefebvre in Giordano's *Madame Sans-Gêne* and Fernando in Granados' *Goyescas.* 211. GIOVANNI MARTINELLI as Arnold in Rossini's *Guillaume Tell,* with Rosa Ponselle (see No. 288) as Mathilde.

212

213

214

212. GIULIO CRIMI (1885–1939), Italian tenor, as Vasco da Gama in Meyerbeer's *L'Africaine*. He created the roles of Luigi in Puccini's *Il Tabarro* and Rinuccio in the same composer's *Gianni Schicchi*. 213. MABEL GARRISON (1866–1963), American coloratura soprano, as the Queen of the Night in Mozart's *Die Zauberflöte*. She was at the Met from 1913 to 1920. (Photo: Mishkin, N.Y.) 214. NINON VALLIN (1886–1961), French soprano. Dividing her career between Paris and Buenos Aires, she was one of the greatest French sopranos of her generation. 215. ELISABETH SCHUMANN (1885–1952), German coloratura soprano, as Sophie in Strauss's *Der Rosenkavalier*, one of her most famous roles. This star of the Vienna Opera (1919–1938) was also a great singer of lieder.

222

223

224

225

226

223. LOTTE LEHMANN (1888–1976), German soprano, as the Marschallin in Strauss's *Der Rosenkavalier*. After 20 years in Vienna, where she created the role of the Dyer's Wife in Strauss's *Die Frau ohne Schatten*, she triumphed at the Met from 1934 to 1945. (Photo: Apeda, N.Y.) 224. LOTTE LEHMANN as Elisabeth in Wagner's *Tannhäuser*. (Photo: Setzer, Vienna) 225. LOTTE LEHMANN as Elsa in Wagner's *Lohengrin*. (Photo: Setzer, Vienna) 226. LOTTE LEHMANN as Sieglinde in Wagner's *Die Walküre*.

227

228

229

230

227. FRIDA LEIDER (1888–1975), German soprano, as Brünnhilde in Wagner's *Die Walküre*. Generally considered the greatest Wagnerian dramatic soprano of her generation, she was most closely associated with the Berlin Opera. 228. ANNA FITZIU (1888–1967), American soprano. She sang at the Met in 1916, creating the role of Rosario in Granados' *Goyescas*. (Photo: Mishkin, N.Y.) 229. ALFRED JERGER (born 1889), Austrian bass-baritone (born Brno). He sang at the Vienna Staatsoper from 1921 into the 1950s, and was its director briefly after World War II. He created the role of Mandryka in Strauss's *Arabella*. (Photo: Dietrich, Vienna) 230. GIACOMO RIMINI (1888–1952), Italian baritone, perhaps as Posa in Verdi's *Don Carlo*. This singer, husband of the soprano Rosa Raisa (see No. 265), created the role of Ping in Puccini's *Turandot*. He was with the Chicago Opera from 1916 to 1937. (Photo: Ermini, Milan)

231. HEINRICH SCHLUSNUS (1888–1952), German baritone. Not only one of the greatest German singers of lieder in his day, he was also with the Berlin Opera from 1917 to 1945.

232

232. FRIEDRICH SCHORR (1888–1953), Hungarian baritone, as Wotan in Wagner's *Das Rheingold* or *Die Walküre*. At the Met from 1924 to 1943, he was the most important Wagnerian baritone of the time.

233

234

235

233. CLAUDIA MUZIO (1889–1936), Italian soprano, in the title role of Puccini's *La Tosca*. Her brilliant career included five years at the Met (1916–1921) and ten in Chicago (1922–1932). (Photo: Mishkin, N.Y.) 234. CLAUDIA MUZIO wearing the wreath of Norma (Bellini). 235. CLAUDIA MUZIO as Giorgetta in Puccini's *Il Tabarro*, a role she created. (Photo: White, N.Y.)

236

236. (DAME) MAGGIE TEYTE (Margaret Tate, 1889–1976), English soprano. At the Opéra-Comique 1908–1910, Chicago 1911–1914, Boston 1915–1917, she also specialized in the French art song.

244

245

246

245. BENIAMINO GIGLI (1890–1957), Italian tenor. The most famous Italian tenor after Caruso, he created the role of Flammen in Mascagni's *Lodoletta.* 246. BENIAMINO GIGLI as Des Grieux in Massenet's *Manon.*

247

248

247. LAURITZ MELCHIOR (1893–1973), Danish heroic tenor, as Siegfried in Wagner's *Die Götterdämmerung*. The most celebrated Wagnerian tenor of this century (he began as a baritone), he had a phenomenal worldwide career, appearing at the Met from 1926 to 1950. 248. LAURITZ MELCHIOR as Tristan in Wagner's *Tristan und Isolde*.

249

249. MARIA IVOGÜN (Ilse von Günther, born 1891), Austrian coloratura soprano (born Budapest). She enjoyed great success in Europe and America. (Photo: Leopold, Munich)

250

250. ALEXANDER KIPNIS (born 1891), Ukrainian bass, as Sarastro in Mozart's *Die Zauberflöte*. His exceptional career culminated in engagements at the Met from 1940 to 1952.

251

251. JOHN CHARLES THOMAS (1891–1960), American baritone, as Germont in Verdi's *La Traviata*. He was at the Met 1934–1943. 252. ANTONIO CORTIS (1891–1952), Spanish tenor, as Alfredo in Verdi's *La Traviata*. He sang in Chicago 1924–1932. (Photo: Daguerre, Chicago) 253. EMANUEL LIST (1891–1967), Austrian bass, as Pogner in Wagner's *Die Meistersinger von Nürnberg*. He was with the Berlin Opera 1924–1934 and with the Met 1934–1949. 254. MARIO CHAMLEE (Archer Cholmondeley, 1892–1966), American tenor, as Cavaradossi in Puccini's *La Tosca*. He sang at the Met 1920–1928 and 1936–1939. 255. MARIO BASIOLA (1892–1965), Italian baritone. At the Met 1925–1931, he later was highly successful in Italy. (Photo: Mishkin, N.Y., autographed 1926)

252

253

254

255

256

257

258

256. GIACOMO LAURI-VOLPI (born 1892), Italian tenor, as Radames in Verdi's *Aïda*. One of the most important twentieth-century Italian tenors, he sang at the Met 1923–1933. (Photo: Mishkin, N.Y.) 257. BENVENUTO FRANCI (born 1892), Italian baritone, as Fanuel in Boito's *Nerone*. He starred at La Scala from 1923 into the 1940s. (Photo: Castagneri, Milan) 258. IRENE MINGHINI-CATTANEO (1892–1944), Italian mezzo-soprano. Her career was in Europe and South America. (Photo: Castagneri, Milan)

259

260

261

262

259. EZIO PINZA (1892–1957), Italian bass, in the title role of Mozart's *Don Giovanni.* Principal bass at the Met from 1926 to 1948, he was also extremely successful in his European appearances. 260. EZIO PINZA as Méphistophélès in Gounod's *Faust*. 261. EZIO PINZA in the title role of Boito's *Mefistofele*. 262. EZIO PINZA early in his career in the title role of Mozart's *Don Giovanni*.

263

263. RICHARD TAUBER (1892–1948), Austrian tenor. Immensely popular in grand opera, operetta and film, he created the tenor roles in several works by Lehár. (Photo: Schneider, Berlin)

264

264. (DAME) EVA TURNER (born 1892), English soprano, as Brünnhilde in Wagner's *Siegfried*. Chiefly associated with the opera houses of Italy, she also sang in England, Germany, the United States and South America.

265

265. ROSA RAISA (1893–1963), Polish soprano. A star of the Chicago Opera from 1916 into the 1930s, she also appeared with great success around the world. She created the role of Asteria in Boito's *Nerone* and the title role of Puccini's *Turandot*. (Photo: Matzene, Chicago) 266. ROSA RAISA in the title role of Mascagni's *Isabeau*. (Photo: Burke-Atwell, Chicago, 1918)

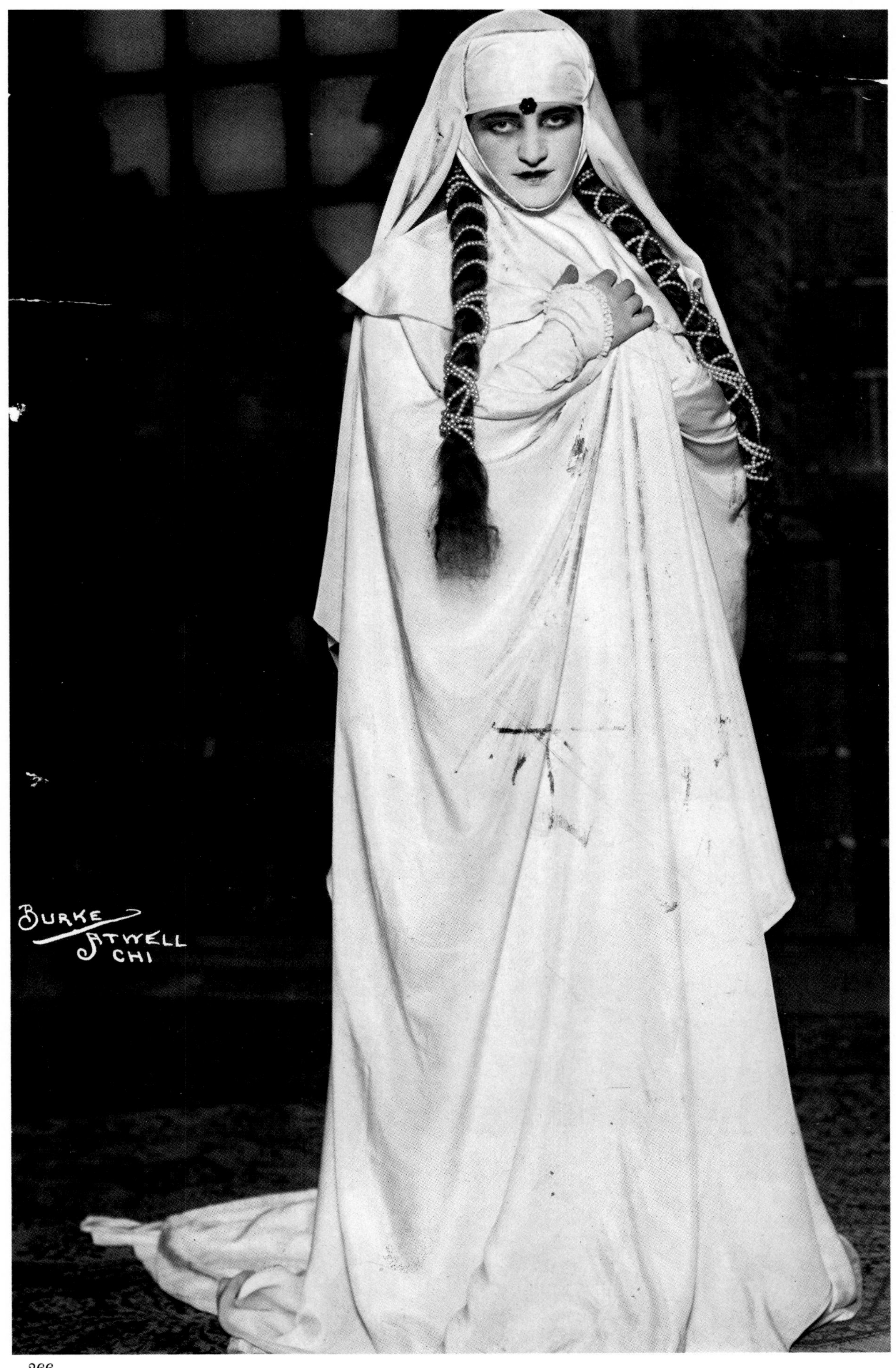

266

267

267. TANCREDI PASERO (born 1893), Italian bass. His 40-year European and American career included the years 1929–1934 at the Met. 268. FLORENCE AUSTRAL (Florence Wilson, 1894–1968), Australian soprano. Chiefly associated with Covent Garden from the early 1920s to 1940, she specialized in Wagner.

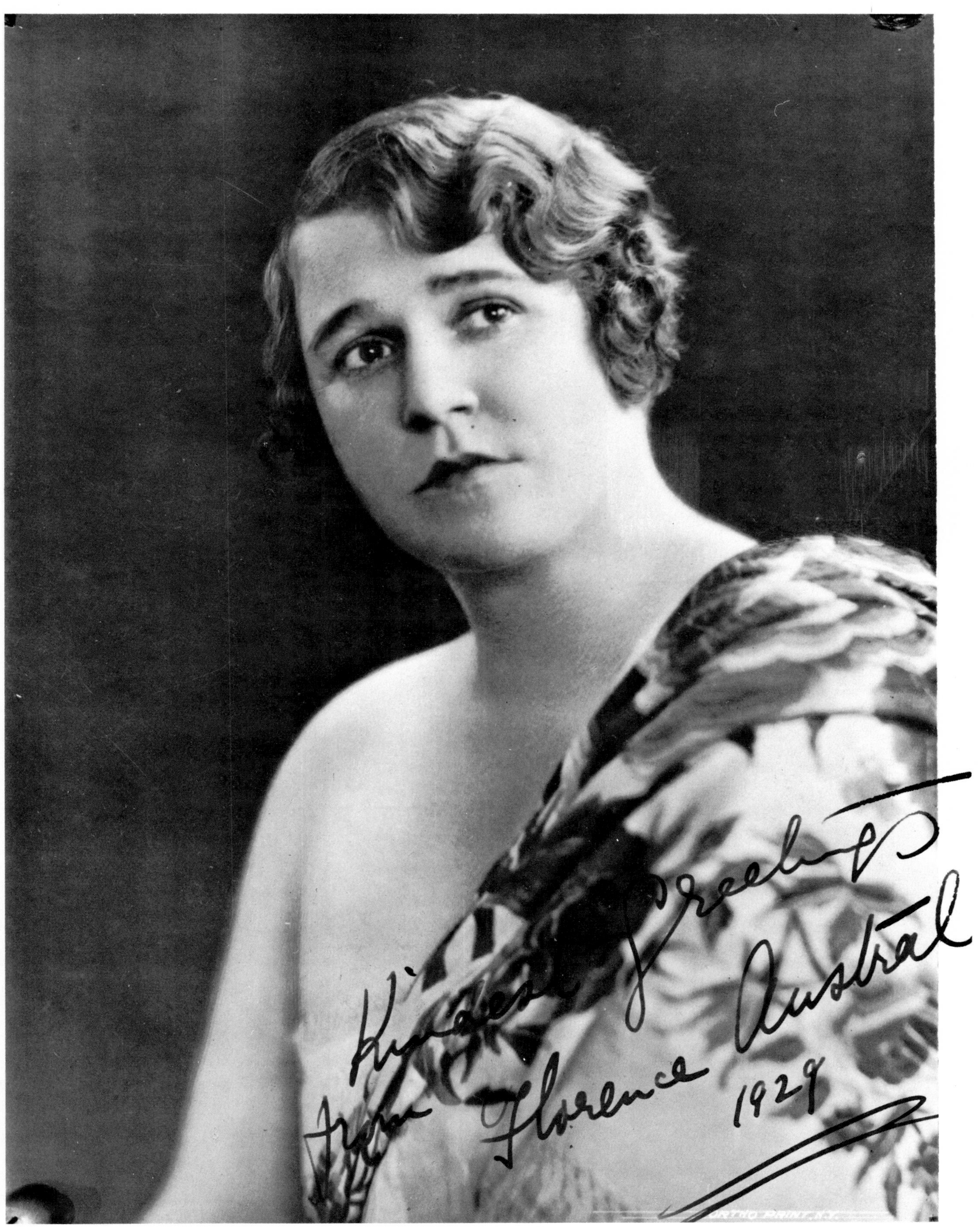
Kindest Greetings
from Florence Austral
1929

268

275

276

275. ELISABETH RETHBERG (Lisbeth Sättler, 1894–1976), German soprano, in the title role of Puccini's *Madama Butterfly*. She starred at the Met 1922–1942. Toscanini called her the perfect soprano. (Photo: Mishkin) 276. ELISABETH RETHBERG as Sieglinde in Wagner's *Die Walküre*.

277

278

279

277. KIRSTEN FLAGSTAD (1895–1962), Norwegian soprano, as Isolde in Wagner's *Tristan und Isolde*. One of the very great Wagnerian singers of the century, she was at the Met 1935–1941 and 1952, and was director of the Oslo Opera from 1958 to 1960. 278. KIRSTEN FLAGSTAD as Brünnhilde in Wagner's *Die Walküre*. 279. KIRSTEN FLAGSTAD as Elsa in Wagner's *Lohengrin*.

280

281

282

280. LUDWIG HOFMANN (1895–1964), German bass, as Wotan in Wagner's *Das Rheingold* or *Die Walküre*. With the Vienna Opera 1935–1942, he appeared at the Met between 1932 and 1938. 281. HANS HERMANN NISSEN (born 1896), German baritone (born Danzig), as Count Almaviva in Mozart's *Le Nozze di Figaro*. He starred at the Munich Opera from 1925 into the 1960s. (Photo: Stiffel, Munich) 282. RENÉ MAISON (1895–1962), Belgian tenor. His long career included engagements in Chicago 1928–1931 and at the Met 1935–1943. (Photo: Apers, Paris)

283

283. CONCHITA SUPERVÍA (1895–1936), Spanish mezzo-soprano, as Hänsel in Humperdinck's *Hänsel und Gretel.* Most famous for her revival of the Rossini coloratura mezzo roles, she sang at Chicago 1915–1920. (Photo: Castagneri, Milan)

284

285

284. KERSTIN THORBORG (born 1896), Swedish mezzo-soprano, as Orfeo in Gluck's *Orfeo ed Euridice*. She sang at the Met from 1936 to 1950. 285. JOSÉ MOJICA (1896–1975), Mexican tenor. He sang with the Chicago Opera 1919–1930 and 1940, and starred in musical films.

To
James Camner
Rosa Ponselle
1976
as
"Gioconda"
C
MISHKIN
NY 80

288

289

290

288. ROSA PONSELLE (Rosa Ponzillo, born 1897), American soprano, in the title role of Ponchielli's *La Gioconda*. She starred at the Met from 1918 to 1936. (Photo: Mishkin, N.Y.) 289. ROSA PONSELLE as Rachel in Halévy's *La Juive*. (Photo: Mishkin, N.Y.) 290. ROSA PONSELLE as Violetta in Verdi's *La Traviata*. (Photo: Mishkin, N.Y.) See also No. 211.

291

292

291. TOTI DAL MONTE (Antonietta Meneghelli, 1898–1976), Italian soprano, in Giordano's *Il Rè* (she created the role). Her important career included the 1924/1925 season at the Met and years 1924–1928 in Chicago. She was briefly married to the tenor Enzo de Muro Lomanto (see No. 303). (Photo: Castagneri, Milan) 292. TOTI DAL MONTE in the title role of Donizetti's *Lucia di Lammermoor*. (Photo: Camuzzi, for Crimella, Milan)

293

294

293. MARIA MÜLLER (1898–1958), German soprano (born Bohemia). She sang at the Met from 1925 to 1935, specializing in Wagner. (Photo: Elzin, N.Y.)
294. EDITHA FLEISCHER (born 1898), German coloratura soprano. She was at the Met 1926–1936, at the Teatro Colón 1936–1949.

162

295

296

295. HELEN TRAUBEL (1899–1972), American soprano, as Isolde in Wagner's *Tristan und Isolde*. With the Met 1937–1953, she became their leading Wagnerian soprano during Flagstad's absence. 296. HELEN TRAUBEL (Photo: Abresch, N.Y.)

299

300

299. JOHN BROWNLEE (1900–1969), Australian baritone, as Amfortas in Wagner's *Parsifal*. Already famous at Glyndebourne and elsewhere, he was with the Met 1937–1953 and then became director of the Manhattan Institute of Music.
300. ERNA BERGER (born 1900), German coloratura soprano. She was with the Berlin Opera from 1934 into the 1950s and appeared at the Met 1949–1951.

301

302

303

304

301. GRACE MOORE (1901–1947), American soprano, in the title role of Charpentier's *Louise*. In addition to her musical-comedy and film work, this popular soprano was at the Met from 1928 to 1932 and from 1934 until her death. 302. RICHARD CROOKS (born 1900), American tenor. After successes in Europe, he sang at the Met 1933–1946. 303. ENZO DE MURO LOMANTO (Vincenzo de Muro, 1902–1952), Italian tenor, in Giordano's *Il Rè* (he created the role). His career was chiefly in Italy. He was married to Toti Dal Monte (see No. 291). (Photo: Castagneri, Milan) 304. JAN KIEPURA (1902–1966), Polish tenor. At the Met 1938–1942, he also appeared in films and operettas. (Photo: Willinger, Vienna)

305

306

307

305. BIDÚ SAYÃO (Balduina Sayão, born 1902), Brazilian soprano, as Violetta in Verdi's *La Traviata*. She starred at the Met 1937–1952. 306. CHARLES KULLMAN (born 1903), American tenor, as Rodolfo in Puccini's *La Bohème*. He was with the Met from 1935 to 1956. (Photo: Willinger) 307. MARGARETE KLOSE (1902–1968), German contralto, as Waltraute in Wagner's *Die Götterdämmerung*. She was with the Berlin Opera 1928–1949 and 1958–1961.

308

317

318

319

317. AULIKKI RAUTAWAARA (born 1906), Finnish soprano. Her European career included famous seasons at Glyndebourne. (Photo: Otto Dyar) 318. ALESSANDRO ZILIANI (born 1906), Italian tenor, as Pinkerton in Puccini's *Madama Butterfly*. His career was largely in Italy. He was briefly married to the soprano Mafalda Favero (see No. 314). 319. ALEXANDER SVÉD (born 1906), Hungarian baritone. He sang at the Met from 1940 to 1950.

320

321

320. JARMILA NOVOTNÁ (born 1907), Bohemian soprano. With the Vienna Opera 1933–1938 (she created the title role in Lehár's *Giuditta*), she was at the Met 1940–1957. (Photo: Bull) 321. LINA BRUNA-RASA (born 1907), Italian soprano, in Wolf-Ferrari's *Sly* (she created the main female role). Her career was chiefly associated with La Scala. (Photo: Castagneri, Milan)

322

322. JUSSI BJÖRLING (1907–1960), Swedish tenor (center), with Leonard Warren (see No. 330) and ZINKA MILANOV (born 1906), Croatian soprano, at an RCA recording session. Björling, one of the truly great twentieth-century tenors, was at the Met 1938–1941 and from 1946 until his death. Milanov joined the Met in 1937 and enjoyed great success there for over 20 years.

323

324

325

323. ROSE BAMPTON (born 1908), American soprano, as Donna Anna in Mozart's *Don Giovanni.* Beginning as a mezzo-soprano, she sang at the Met from 1932 to 1950. (Photo: Abresch, N.Y.) 324. IRRA PETINA (born 1907), Russian-American soprano, as Fyodor in Mussorgsky's *Boris Godunov.* She sang at the Met from 1933 to 1944. 325. BRUNA CASTAGNA (born 1908), Italian mezzo-soprano, in the title role of Bizet's *Carmen,* her most famous part. She was at the Met from 1936 to 1945. (Photo: Abresch, N.Y.) 326. MARJORIE LAWRENCE (born 1909), Australian soprano. Her magnificent career, which included the years 1932–1935 at the Paris Opéra and 1935–1941 at the Met, was interrupted and curtailed by polio.

326

327

327. HANS HOTTER (born 1909), German bass-baritone, as Jokanaan in Strauss's *Salome*. A leading opera and concert star of the century, he sang at the Met from 1950 to 1954. 328. LINA PAGLIUGHI (born 1910), coloratura soprano (born San Francisco to Italian parents). Her brilliant career was chiefly in Europe and South America, with tours in North America.

328

329

329. MARIA CEBOTARI (1910–1949), Bessarabian soprano, in the title role of Puccini's *Madama Butterfly*. Her varied European opera and film career ended with her Vienna Opera engagement from 1943 until her death.

330

330. LEONARD WARREN (1911–1960), American baritone, as Tonio in Leoncavallo's *I Pagliacci*. He was a leading baritone at the Met from 1939 until his death. See also No. 322.

331

332

331. FERRUCCIO TAGLIAVINI (born 1913), Italian tenor. His truly international career included the years 1946–1950 at the Met. 332. MILIZA KORJUS (born 1912), American (allegedly Polish) soprano, in the 1938 film *The Great Waltz*. She made guest appearances at several European opera houses. (Photo: Apger)

333

334

333. LICIA ALBANESE (born 1913), Italian soprano. She sang at the Met from 1940 into the 1960s. (Photo: Bruno of Hollywood, N.Y.) 334. LICIA ALBANESE as Violetta in Verdi's *La Traviata*.

335

335. LJUBA WELITSCH (Ljuba Velitchkova, born 1913), Bulgarian soprano, in the title role of Strauss's *Salome*, her most famous part. After many successes in Europe, she appeared at the Met from 1948 into the 1950s. 336. BLANCHE THEBOM (born 1918), American mezzo-soprano, in the title role of Bizet's *Carmen*. She was a leading singer at the Met from 1944 until well into the 1960s. (Photo: Bender)

336

337

337. RISË STEVENS (born 1913), American mezzo-soprano. She starred at the Met from 1939 to 1964. (Photo: Heinrich) 338. RICHARD TUCKER (1913–1975), American tenor, in the title role of Giordano's *Andrea Chenier*. He was one of the leading Met tenors from 1945 until his death. (Photo: Le Blang)

338

339

339. ELEANOR STEBER (born 1916), American soprano. With the Met from 1940, she created the title role in Barber's *Vanessa.* (Photo: Bruno of Hollywood, N.Y.)

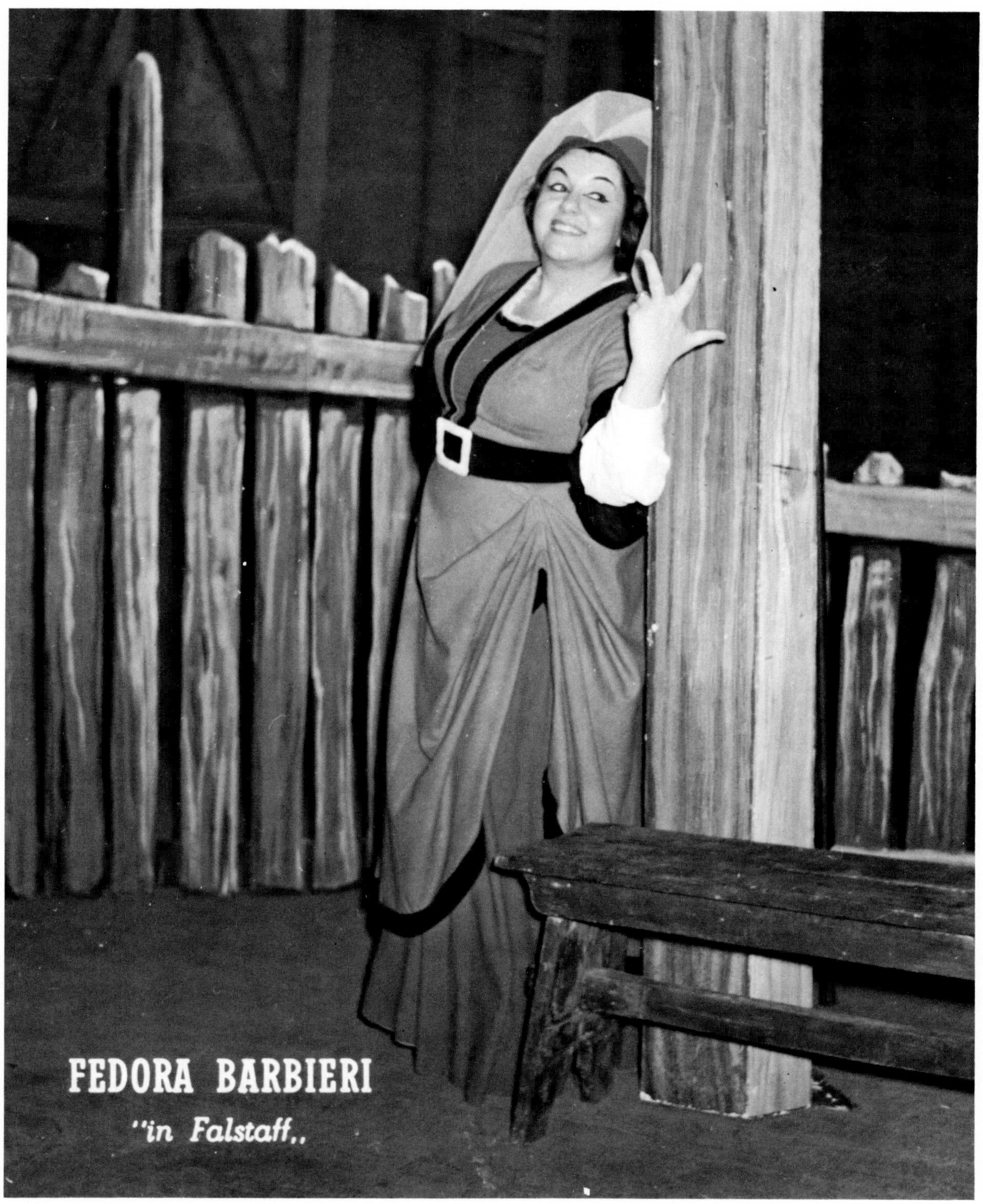

340

340. FEDORA BARBIERI (born 1920), Italian mezzo-soprano, as Dame Quickly in Verdi's *Falstaff*. A brilliant European career led to her 1952 engagement with the Met.

341

341. TITO GOBBI (born 1915), Italian baritone, in the title role of Verdi's *Falstaff*. With La Scala from 1942, he has appeared around the world to great acclaim. (Photo: Times, London)

342

342. RAMÓN VINAY (born 1914), Chilean heroic tenor (also sang baritone roles), in the title role of Verdi's *Otello*, his best part. He joined the Met in 1946.

INDEX

Surnames beginning with the elements d', de, De and von are listed under the element that follows these. References are to figure numbers rather than page numbers.